The Giving Heart

Unlocking the Transformative Power
of Generosity in Our Lives

M. J. Ryan

foreword by Sylvia Boorstein

CONARI PRESS
Berkeley, California

Conari Press books are distributed by Publishers Group West.

ISBN: 1-57324-521-6

Cover Illustration: Roger Montoya
Cover Art Direction: Ame Beanland
Book Design: Suzanne Albertson

LIBRARY OF CONGRESS CATALOGING-IN-PUBLICATION DATA
Ryan, M. J. (Mary Jane), 1952-
The giving heart : unlocking the transformative power of generosity
in your life / M.J. Ryan; foreword by Sylvia Boorstein.
p.   cm.
Includes bibliographical references.
ISBN 1-57324-521-6
1. Generosity. I. Title.
BJ1533.G4 R93 2000
177'.7—dc21
00-009922

Printed in the United States of America on recycled paper.
00 01 02 03   RRD NW   10 9 8 7 6 5 4 3 2 1

In honor of
all my teachers
of the heart,
particularly my father

*We make a living by what we get, but we
make a life by what we give.*

—NORMAN MACESWAN

5

An Ever~Expanding Circle 161

The Giving Heart

1

Opening Our Hearts and Hands 1

2

The Gifts of Giving 11

3

The Spirit of Giving 45

4

The Practice of Giving 95

The Giving Heart

3

The Spirit of Giving 45

4
The Practice of Giving 95

5

An Ever~Expanding Circle 161